T]

Irresistible

Qualities Men

Want In A

Woman

What High-Quality Men *Secretly* Look
For When Choosing "The One"

By Bruce Bryans

Legal Disclaimer

Although the information in this book may be very useful, it is sold with the understanding that neither the author nor the publisher is engaged in presenting specific psychological, emotional, or sexual advice. Nor is anything in this book intended to be a diagnosis, prescription, recommendation, or cure for any specific kind of psychological, emotional, or sexual problem. Each person has unique needs and this book cannot take these individual differences into account.

ISBN-13: 978-1494286804

ISBN-10: 1494286807

Introduction

I'll be honest. I'm a man, and therefore I can only tell you with complete certainty how men think and what we want. Yes, I do consider myself a "quality" guy, but I'm acquainted with myself well enough to know that I'm not perfect. No man is. So what makes me so special that I can tell you what good men secretly want in a woman? Well, I have one superpower a good majority of men haven't developed quite well...

...I am able to confidently understand and communicate my emotional needs to the opposite sex.

I guess it's one of the benefits of being an introverted, analytical writer.

Now, a good majority of men out there don't know what they secretly crave from a woman on an emotional level and therefore they cannot tell you. On the other hand, you have a handful of guys who do know what they desperately desire in a woman, but they don't know *how* to communicate those needs effectively.

Women only find out the things I'm about to tell you after years of trial and error or by fighting to get a man to finally "open up" about his emotions. Whether it's because of pride, fear of rejection, or even the fear of looking weak and needy, a man will not outright tell you what he needs on that deep, emotional level until he can completely trust you. In short, this book will reveal to you the irresistible qualities that men desire in a woman he wants a RELATIONSHIP with.

This short booklet is all about what a high-quality

man wants in a woman he considers girlfriend or even wife material. Don't worry; I'm not going to cover abstract ideas and the nuanced tastes of every man, because quite frankly, different men want very different things. For instance, some men want a woman who's athletic, some guys prefer scholarly women, and others love a domesticated, future homemaker as their ideal woman.

Again, these are differences in taste that no single source of information can account for. However, even though different men want different things, we can agree that ALL men prefer being with a woman who possesses certain qualities of <u>character</u> and <u>personality</u> that make her stand out amongst her peers.

Even more so, high-quality men have a higher standard than the average Joe. And because of this high standard, men like this are usually aware that they have a wider pool of women to choose from. Let me make this clear: a high-quality man who knows what he wants and who is comfortable asserting himself to get his needs met will NOT settle for just any woman to build a meaningful relationship with. Men like this want a woman who exudes high character, and though she may be beautiful on the outside, he expects her <u>inner worth</u> to be far superior to the women around her. Ask any man (good man) you know and he'll agree with me on this.

What High-Quality Men Want in a Woman

I should mention that this booklet isn't going to tell you anything about the average man. This is a book about HIGH-QUALITY men. These are the assertive, strong-willed, compassionate, and committed men in society. They are the strong, the leaders, and the few among many. These are the men that other men look up to and that most women secretly want to be with. And if you have no idea what these men look for in a life partner…then this book is for you.

I'll admit that I cannot tell you if the man you desire wants large breasted, small breasted, tall, or short women. However, I can tell you exactly what qualities of a woman's **character** that this kind of man finds irresistible, indispensible, and irreplaceable. I can tell you the inner qualities that can make the RIGHT man fall in love with you, but I cannot tell you what every man's ideal "type" of woman is.

In short, once you pass a good man's "physical appearance" test that is specific to *his tastes*, it's your inner value (or lack thereof) that will either lose or keep his interest in you. Believe it or not, a lot of women disqualify (yes…disqualify) themselves from relationships with good men because of negative inner qualities that they have failed to get a hold on. On the other hand, if you develop the irresistible qualities in this book, you might find yourself attracting men who normally don't date "your type." These qualities make a woman attractive regardless of her physical beauty.

Deserving What You Want

Deserving what you want is one of the core concepts I teach guys when it comes to attracting a quality woman and building a relationship with her. I say this to point out that my advice isn't one-sided.

Because this is a book for women, obviously I'm focusing on how a woman can develop qualities that a man finds attractive. When I write for men, I tell them the exact same thing. In short, I don't expect any woman who reads this book to settle for a man who doesn't exude high character. Work on deserving what you want and you'll attract a man who is worth your time.

Now, as you read through each chapter and observe the inner qualities that men find attractive I want you to keep in mind that I'm not proposing perfection. Even your "knight-in-shining-armor" is prone to bouts of insanity and less than virtuous behavior, but his imperfections should not bring down his overall character. How often you show these qualities of character is more important than how well you do them. Good men aren't looking for perfection; they just want to know that they've found something special in a sea of mediocre women.

I must also admit that the qualities I'm about to mention will make you reassess your behavior and compel you to strive for a higher standard from yourself. That's exactly what I want you to do; because it's the striving for a higher standard that makes a woman praiseworthy and irresistibly attractive to a quality man. Remember that.

With all that said, I must regrettably admit that this book isn't for everyone. Here are two ways to know if this book will benefit you or not:

1. You want to attract and keep a high-quality man (a man with high self-esteem, ambition, leadership qualities, compassion, cherishes commitment, has high-standards for himself, defends his personal boundaries,

knows what he wants, speaks his mind, understands the value of relationships, and exudes masculine, sexual confidence).

2. You want to pursue and nurture a *long-term relationship* with such a man.

If you're not interested in guys that will hold you to a high but reasonable standard (meaning he won't tolerate flaky or disrespectful behavior) or if you're not interested in long-term relationships with masculine men who value commitment…this book is not for you. If you want to attract one-night stands, so called "players", or forty something year-old bad boys who think commitment is just another curse word…this book is not for you. However, if you want to draw the attention of high-quality men and be perceived as the most favorable woman for a long-term relationship filled with love, trust, passion, and commitment, then I encourage you to read on.

Table of Contents

Chapter 1:

A Woman's Most Attractive Quality...

1

Honesty

A Woman's Best Quality

Let me be blunt here for a minute…

Great guys do not want to build relationships with dishonest women. And ALL of my guy friends who are either married or in a serious relationship will tell you the same thing. Frankly, if you want to make a man fall in love with you, be completely honest and upfront with him about who you are, what you're all about, and what you want out of life. Don't be something you're not just to appease him.

In the sub sections below I talk about specific aspects of honesty and what men find attractive about it. But if I could sum it all up in one sentence it would be this…

Don't be deceitful.

Stupidly obvious isn't it? If it is, I apologize for insulting your intelligence. But before you start throwing stones at me, read on to see how men perceive honesty in a woman and how women sometimes use deceit in unattractive ways.

Unlimited Honesty with Limited Openness

Now, being honest doesn't mean that when you first meet a guy you need to tell him everything about your past. It's strange; men want honest women, but not necessarily "open" women. Let me explain. You see, if a man is just getting to know you better but you're too much of an open book, meaning, you reveal everything about yourself too soon, you'll either scare him away or he'll lose interest. Telling him the dark secrets about your past, your family, and that you've gotten back together with your ex-boyfriend more times than you can count doesn't make you look endearing…it makes you look crazy. This kind of honesty is what I like to call too-much-information-way-too-quickly, and MOST guys don't like it. To them, you may come off as a bit of a nut job, because everything you tell him is being evaluated by his limited experience with you.

When a man has the opportunity to observe your behavior he makes his own estimation of the kind of woman you are now, in the present, regardless of what you say about your past. If you tell him everything way too early, he'll be forced to make snap judgments about you now, in the present, based on what you say. Be mysterious and give him the opportunity to unravel the mystery that is you, but if he asks…always, always, be honest. Sometimes being mysterious can be a bit more fun and romantic, especially if he likes a challenge.

Also, being mysterious helps to keep the passion alive in your relationship. Psychologist and best-selling author, Esther Perel, is recognized as one of the world's most respected researchers on relationships and sexuality. In one of her TEDTalks, she mentions that novelty and privacy are two key components for ensuring that there's enough mystery in a relationship to keep the sparks of passion going. She mentions that not knowing everything about your partner (and vice versa) will help to maintain higher levels of desire.

Passion is fed by our desire, or put another way…we *want* to *want*. So if you want to keep a man interested in you, learn how to be honest with him but allow him the opportunity to *crave* getting to know you. By being mysterious you become much more desirable, therefore making yourself an irresistible catch that a man *wants* to pursue. In short, by being mysterious to a man you actually give him the gift of seducing you.

For a lot of women, maintaining their mystery is especially difficult because when they find a good man they want to do whatever they can to keep him. They become easily accessible, sexually available, and completely open. In the end, even a great guy with good intentions can lose interest in a woman who's too open and too available. Why? Because to him, she has no more mystery left to her since she revealed too much of herself too quickly. He may feel cheated out of a challenge and your value may actually drop in his eyes.

To a man, a woman's mystery equates to sacred beauty. So if you take nothing else from this book, keep at least this thought with you always: *Cherish your sacred beauty, those things which make you desirable to a man, because the more you cherish it, the more a man will pursue you to discover it and the more he will sacrifice to possess it.*

Trust me on this. I know it sounds counterintuitive, but that's because men act differently than how most women *think* men behave. Chances are, your Mr. McDreamy is going to be most happy if you let him seduce you…slowly. Give him the gift of unraveling you. And remember, always be honest, but try to be as mysterious as you can.

Don't Put On a Façade

Never put on a front with a high-quality guy. As the cliché goes: always be yourself, the best version of that self. Also, be upfront and candid with him as comfortably as you can. It's important to be upfront as early as possible because the real you will come out eventually. Being honest with him from the beginning will cause him to have a higher level of RESPECT for you. And if you so happen to be honest and upfront with a guy and he doesn't respect you for it, simply move on. Any guy who can't accept you being yourself and having your own set of standards and beliefs is obviously not a good match for you.

Men who have high-standards and integrity do not enjoy the intimate company of women who manipulate the truth to get what they want. And no good man in his right mind will want to pursue a relationship with a woman who turned out to be something completely different from what he thought she was.

For example, sometimes fate may have it that you'll meet Mr. McDreamy while you're on the tail end of a dead relationship. If you already have a boyfriend, it's important that you make that clear. It's understandable if things aren't working out in your present relationship and you're ready to move on, just be mature about it. You'd be surprised just how understanding (and competitive) men can be with a woman who's in an unhappy relationship. Tell him that you have a boyfriend but it's not working out and that you're looking for something more.

Whatever you do, just don't lie to Mr. McDreamy, because if he does find out that you had a boyfriend while you started dating him, his trust in you might diminish greatly. If you tell him about your situation and he still sticks around but gives you room to transition into singlehood again, that's great. On the other hand, if he doesn't want to be the catalyst to an inevitable breakup, that's great as well. Let him lead, and don't try to manipulate a situation with dishonesty just to get a man...ever.

So remember, be yourself, always be truthful, and let the chips fall where they may.

Don't Play Games if He's Leading

Let's say that you've met a great guy and it's become ridiculously obvious that he's taken an interest in you. While tons of dating books will tell you to play hard-to-get, consider that tons of women read those books and are still single, or at least end up with men who waste their precious time. If a man is seriously interested in you and he's making his intentions clear...do not play hard-to-get.

Now, later as your relationship develops there may come a time when you'll have to take your foot off the gas and pull away from him if you see that he's beginning to lose interest in you or if he begins to take you for granted. This usually happens when you give him all your focus and attention. When that time comes, then you pull out your subtle moves of seduction to draw him back in.

But when you notice a man *taking the lead* to get your attention, you give him that attention. Notice what I said… "When you notice a man taking the lead." What this means is that he should be initiating the relationship and making the moves necessary to cultivate intimacy. When you see him going out of his way to get to know you better, be upfront and honest with him…don't play games.

On Being Vulnerable

Being honest with a man also means that you're capable of being vulnerable with him. I'll be the first to admit that at the end of the day, men don't really want some superwoman who's so perfect that she cannot fail. That's not what this book of virtuous and attractive qualities is all about, which is why I had to mention this early on and why it's important to a man.

Men truly want an *emotional experience* with a great woman, and he can only enjoy this level of intimacy when a woman is vulnerable with him. You have to be willing to display weakness, failure, insecurity, and even your ugly side *without shame or regret*. If a man can stand firm as your emotions wash over him, he's worth your time. Even more so, if he connects with your vulnerability by showing you his own, he's probably a keeper.

As human beings, we're strong not because we don't display pain and weakness, but when we can put it out there for the world to see and be indifferent to what people think of us. And when it comes to relating with men, a man enjoys being in a position to lend strength to his woman. **Feminine vulnerability awakens the masculine spirit**.

A woman that bares her wounds at the appropriate time in a relationship gives a man the perfect opportunity to protect, defend, nurture, and love. Men aren't quick to show their emotional wounds, no matter how old or far in the past they may be, but when a woman can be vulnerable with him he has the opportunity to show her both his strength and his weaknesses. Read that last paragraph again.

Chapter 2:

That Thing That Makes Her Irreplaceable...

2

Supportiveness

Display the Qualities of an Irreplaceable First Mate

A great guy, who knows what he wants out of life and is on his path to get it isn't just looking for any kind of woman to build a relationship with. No. Men like this want to spend their time with a woman who will be a support for them on their life's journey. If you really want a man to fall in love with you, take this advice to heart:

Do things to show your support for his dreams, goals, and ambitions. If you take a genuine interest in his success and well-being, you become invaluable to him.

A great guy wants to know that you're capable of being the support he needs as he works and perseveres to make his dreams a reality. In fact, he doesn't just want a woman who can encourage him to bring out his fullest potential...he needs it. The more you become one of his main "go-to" sources for inspiration and encouragement, the more he will see you as an indispensible part of his life.

A quality guy is usually a man with a plan, a dream, or some sort of ideal that he wants to live up to.

He needs a woman by his side that can be a source of strength during tough times and a companion to celebrate with during the good times.

A Cry For Love and Respect

Have you ever heard a man complain that you're just not supportive enough? It's a cry for love, which in a man's mind translates to *respect*. For example, if he doesn't feel that you support his desire to become an entrepreneur, he won't feel that you respect his decision to do so.

While it's true that you won't necessarily agree with everything a man does, it's important to show your concern with respect. It's also important to discern when it's okay to let go and just be supportive of him. Remember: let go and let him lead. When a man feels the unshakable support of a good woman, he feels invincible. Your support of his endeavors is a display of unconditional respect, which translates into love.

Support in Word and Action

I can honestly say that one of the things that helped me make the decision to marry my wife was her support. I've always had big dreams and ambitions and I knew that some types of women might not be onboard with some of them. As we dated, I got comfortable talking about my goals and dreams and she was quite supportive of them.

Now when I say supportive, I don't just mean lip service. Of course she said things like, "Hey babe, I'm with you one-hundred percent on this", but she also

DID things to make my goals a reality. She would take the initiative and go out of her way to assist me with those things she knew I needed help with. This is support in action, and unless the guy you're interested in is a completely selfish idiot with an overweening sense of entitlement, he'll be deeply grateful and moved by your devotion.

Be Genuinely Interested in Him

A great way a woman shows her support for her man is by being genuinely interested in his success, desires, and well-being. If you can become genuinely interested in your guy, you're on the right path. This single idea can keep a guy magnetized to you simply because you'll be deeply interested in his most favorite thing in the world…himself.

Men love it when a woman takes a natural and genuine interest in their lives. A man loves to have his ego stroked by the idea of having a woman take an interest in his success, his dreams, his family, and his life in general. This is quite natural and it's quite okay.

As human beings, we all crave attention in some way, shape, or form. We all desire to be understood by others, and when we find that one person who just "gets us" we'll cling to them like there's no tomorrow. This is why it's so important to learn what makes your guy tick.

Take an interest in him simply by listening to him. Allow him to talk about himself by asking him interesting questions pertaining to his life. As your natural interest in him makes you more interesting to him, he'll begin wanting to spend more and more time with you before he even realizes it.

Becoming His Emotional Backbone

Both men and women have trust issues in relationships, but for men it can be more intense when it comes to trusting themselves totally to women. Men are naturally more guarded about their emotions than women are. Because of this, they have a more difficult time being completely open about their feelings, inner needs, and conflicts.

One of the reasons for this is because a man needs to feel that he can completely trust a woman with the tender sides of himself without thinking that she will perceive him as weak. He fears that she'll think less of him and eventually lose interest in him. The man's need to be perceived as the stronger and more powerful of the two genders is deeply ingrained into his psyche. Thus for most men, they must feel that a woman is completely supportive of them before they can show the softer side of themselves.

By finding unique ways of showing your unwavering support and loyalty, a man can become much more trusting and open with time. Become his one-woman private cheering squad and also his source of nurturing and maternal strength, and he will love you all the more for it.

When You Cannot Support Him

If there's one thing I've learned about women is that when it comes to relating with men...women want *security*. With this in mind, if you're dating a guy and for whatever reason you cannot support some of his life choices, it might be better to leave. Don't put all your hopes on the idea that he *might* change his mind in the future, because quite frankly, he probably won't. You'll be better off finding a man whose work, passions, choice of friends, etc. you can support in the long-run, otherwise, you're just gambling with your future happiness. Don't gamble with your future happiness.

If you find your boyfriend making decisions that cause you to lose sleep at night…he might not be the right guy for you. If you always combat his choices because they seem unreasonable or they make you insecure about your future happiness…he might not be the right guy for you. While it's important to support your man no matter what, if you're in a dating relationship and you feel *threatened* by his goals, ambitions, interests, etc., you need to let him know as early as possible.

Just because you cannot support a man's decision doesn't necessarily mean that he's making a bad choice. We all have different needs and wants in life, and we will come into conflict with the needs and wants of others. If his needs and wants are always in conflict with yours, or if you perceive that it might be in the future…don't waste his time or yours. It might be better to end things early on if you both can't find a reasonable compromise.

Eagerly Support Him But Don't Become His Slave

Here's the thing, men want a supportive woman, but don't fall into the trap of becoming a man's slave.

What I mean is that you should always know when enough is enough and don't allow any man to constantly take advantage of you. In a healthy relationship, there should be mutual support from both parties. If you find yourself always supporting the things he does but he doesn't prioritize the things that are important to you both now and in the future, let him know how you feel.

It's highly important that you assert yourself and communicate your needs to your man in a graceful way so that he doesn't feel disrespected. You need to have open, respectful communication with a man in order to *influence* him and make him *want* to change for you. Be as supportive as you can, but always respectfully communicate your needs so that he doesn't take you for granted.

Some women are so "nice" that they allow others, both men and women, to walk all over them. This leaves them feeling resentful, misunderstood, and victimized by those around them. You can support a man, and sacrifice for him as long as he is willing to do the same for you.

Don't become his slave, because even a good man might be tempted to take advantage of a highly supportive, sacrificing woman if she doesn't communicate and defend her personal boundaries. Remember: a good man loves a woman with standards and boundaries.

Be a Supporter...Not His Savior

Sometimes the best way you can support a man is by simply being there for him. If he's going through a tough spot in his life and he turns to you for support, don't feel stressed just because your capacity to help him might be limited. Your purpose isn't to be his one-stop shop for advice on his career, business, health, faith, friendships, etc.

It's important for a man to *take responsibility* for his own problems and find solutions to those problems. You're there to help him as he leads, and encourage him to do so. It's okay to be his shoulder to cry and lean on when things get really tough, but be careful not to make yourself his savior.

While most women have an inner desire to help a man succeed, be careful of dating a man who constantly places you in overwhelmingly stressful positions. What I mean is, the more personal problems he has, the tougher it's going to be for you.

In most cases in a relationship, his problems will become your problems as well. If he doesn't take care of his health, it will become your problem. If he doesn't take care of his finances, it will eventually become your problem. If he doesn't know how to make and keep friends, it will become your problem. And if he doesn't know what he wants to do with his life, it will become your problem.

Now, I know life isn't perfect, and even your Mr. McDreamy might have some things in his life that he needs to work on (I mean, who doesn't?). But it is necessary to be completely aware of what you're getting yourself into when you decide to cultivate a relationship with a man.

Keep in mind that to be supportive of a man will require sacrifice. If you know without a shadow of a doubt that you're in no position to support a man with a certain problem, it may be time for you to make an executive decision and find a man you can confidently support.

Like I said before, life throws us all curve balls at times, but that's no reason to make things extra difficult for yourself by trying to be a supportive girlfriend to a man whose problems are just beyond your ability to cope with. It's a harsh reality, but it's important to know your own limitations.

Which brings me back to my original point. It's not your job to "make him a man." You can help him to act like a man by letting him lead, but you're not designed to make him one. If you've done all you can to support a man and he still isn't trying to help himself, save yourself the future headache and leave.

But if a man is *aggressively proactive* about solving his problems, no matter how big they are…he's worth your time. If he's doing nothing but complaining, even after you've provided ample support, it might be time for you to call it quits.

Stress can kill you, seriously. And as much as I love to see a woman stand by a man through his ups and downs, I hate to see a woman waste her life with a man who won't take responsibility for his own life. If you're supporting a man who's been going through hell for a long time, I can't tell you when enough is enough. Only you can answer that question. But I can tell you this: Always ask yourself these two questions:

1. Is he being responsible for his own problems or is he expecting me to save him? And…

2. Have I been truly supportive of him or have I been trying to be his savior?

Support him with all your heart, but don't make him frcc from being responsible. It takes a while to learn the difference, but with experience you'll know whether or not a man sees you as his support or his savior.

Are You a Capable First Mate?

A great guy is going to need a great first mate to build a new life with. If a quality man doesn't feel confident in your ability to "handle things" when he <u>needs</u> you to, he's not going to consider you long-term relationship material. Whether it's street smarts, book smarts, or plain old common sense, a good man needs someone he can *rely* on without having to give it a second thought.

Being a capable woman means that he can rely on your wisdom and intelligence to support him when necessary. Granted, he'll want to *lead* in most cases, but his capacity to lead is somewhat limited if his "first mate" is incapable of following instructions. Hey, I'm just giving a bit of tough love here, and I tell guys the exact same thing.

Can you imagine being in a relationship with a man who can't seem to follow through on the simplest of tasks? Can you imagine trying to cultivate a relationship with a guy who consistently makes bad decisions just because he fails to think things through? It's the same for men.

When your Mr. McDreamy goes about looking for

the right girl, he's going to choose a woman who's dependable because she has a habit of making wise decisions. Once again, I'm not saying that a man wants a perfect specimen of a woman who never makes a mistake, but I think we both can admit to the fact that some people are better decision makers than others.

Simply put, being a reliable and capable support to your man means that you're able to *take* responsibility and follow through without his constant input. When you and your Mr. McDreamy are a perfect match, this is much easier to accomplish. If you find it extremely difficult or challenging to support a man in those areas where he *needs* you, there may be a mismatch in your strengths and weaknesses as a couple. It's important to be honest with yourself and him if he's expecting more than you can handle.

I've probably belabored the point, but it bears repeating: Great guys want women they can rely on, especially when they're not around. The kind of guys I refer to in this book have an innate ability to make accurate judgments about people, sometimes very quickly. And they realize that reliability is a precursor to responsibility. The higher capacity a woman has to undertake various levels of responsibility, the more valuable she is from a *supportive first mate* standpoint.

While I'm not suggesting that you need to have masterful leadership skills or an inner guru sense that gives you access to infinite wisdom, it IS important that you have an interest in your own personal growth. Fortunately, since you're reading this book I can assume that you're a woman who's interested in personal development and bettering yourself, so from my point of view, you've got that covered.

Consider some of the ideas presented in best-selling author, Thomas J. Stanley's book called, The Millionaire Mind. In it he discusses the characteristics, qualities, and habits that many multimillionaires share with one another that contribute to their high levels of success in both business and relationships. Interestingly, in one of the chapters he discusses how choice of spouse played a significant role in explaining these millionaires' ability to enjoy higher levels of success.

Several qualities consistently presented themselves when he asked these millionaires what qualities made them choose their spouse and what qualities contributed to their successful marriages. One of the key traits that initially interested millionaires in their spouses was reliability, and one of the key traits that contributed to their successful marriages was capableness. In fact, qualities such as these were seen as being more valuable than just "physical attraction."

I mention this to point out that the millionaire men that were interviewed could be considered "high-quality" because they enjoy high levels of economic success as well as stable, happy marriages. Men such as these realize that a reliable woman can be counted on to make wise decisions with or without their presence, and that a capable woman makes for an indispensible life partner.

Now, we can agree that a man doesn't have to be a multimillionaire to be considered "high-quality", but there's no denying that the male individuals surveyed for Stanley's book do possess the kind of virtuous qualities (diligence, humility, unselfishness, honesty, self-belief, etc.) that helped them to grow into successful businessmen, professionals, and loving husbands.

Obviously, men like this realized that their future happiness AND future success depended upon choosing a woman who possessed qualities that would make her *essential* to his well-being. It's food for thought.

Chapter 3:

The Quality That Makes Him LOVE Being Around You...

3

Feminine Gracefulness

Masculine Men Love Women Who LOVE Being Women

Listen, I get it. Back in the day, women didn't have a lot of the rights that men had. If you go even further back in history (and even other parts of the world today) women weren't seen as more than mere property for men. I truly understand how far we've come as a society, and I love the fact that over the years women have stood up for their rights as equal citizens in relation to men.

Now, I'm not here to discuss feminist theory, but I will admit that some parts of today's modern-day feminism has created a divide between women. Some (notice I said "some") women who passionately adhere to extreme feminist doctrine believe that the whole idea of what is considered masculine and what is considered feminine is a societal construct. Granted, there are SOME things that society has artificially labeled as either masculine or feminine in order to encourage consumerism or perpetuate a social ideal.

But there are numerous other qualities and behaviors that are built into the male and female psyches that cause us to *naturally* define things as masculine or feminine. Why am I mentioning all of this? I say this to simply stress the point that IF your goal is to attract a mature, masculine man who LOVES the fact that he's a man, you'll have a much easier time going along with *nature* rather than trying to go against her.

You, as a woman have two options when it comes to being attractive to a man. You can fight against *nature* and work your tail off to convince Mr. McDreamy that he should be *attracted* to you based on society's new definition of femininity (or its attempt to redefine it), or you can accept *nature* and work on developing feminine qualities that highly masculine men already consider *attractive*.

The former path will cause you to lose your mind and you might end up settling for a man who probably won't be able to light your fires, if you know what I mean. The latter path is much easier for you as a woman because at the end of the day, you are, by birthright…a woman. In short, high-quality men (who are comfortable in their masculinity) are *naturally attracted* to women who embrace their femininity.

Equal But Different…For Good Reason

No matter how equal men and women are, they are, in fact, still VERY different creatures. I honestly believe that a woman can embrace her femininity and still be considered a man's equal. Men aren't looking for a woman to lord over, control, or dominate (unless you're into that sort of thing). Quality men *prefer* women who love the fact that they were born a woman.

When you look at the differences between the sexes from nature's standpoint, I think we can agree that these differences exist to aid us in the procreation process. I know that this all doesn't sound very "sexy", but consider the idea that it's our gender differences that actually make men want women, and vice versa, because of the desire for sex and love. While we don't have to define masculinity and femininity based on culturally influenced, and often exaggerated stereotypes, we can define them based on what's good for making babies.

For instance, a masculine man has a higher chance of competing with and dominating those around him in order to protect and provide for those under his care. While a feminine woman, on the other hand, has a higher chance of producing and nurturing healthy offspring.

So keep in mind that the very things that make you feminine actually make you irresistibly sexy to men who are unapologetically masculine. But what are those specific qualities that make a woman intrinsically feminine? Here are the most important ones that guys look for in a woman:

Nurturing – Tenderness, kindness, thoughtfulness, and affection are all aspects of a nurturing persona. Men crave the tender touch and warm affection of a woman. This quality is even doubly important because men know, perhaps on an instinctual level, that a nurturing woman has a higher chance of becoming an excellent mother to his children.

Playfulness – Flirtatiousness, humor, and romantic teasing add to a woman's allure. As long as he's the object of your desire, a man loves a flirtatious, playful woman that knows how to stimulate him emotionally.

Mystery – I could write a whole book about how being "mysterious" can drive a man crazy for you (in a good way). A woman's mystery intrigues a man and keeps him coming back for more. Sadly, I honestly feel that in our western society, many women have lost the art of seduction. A woman's mystery is maintained because of her class, elegance, modesty, and her seductive subtlety. But as culture would have it, a lot of women are more aggressive these days and so many have become open books.

I mean, just look at the average Facebook profile. A man can find out more about a woman these days with a quick Google search than through an intimate conversation. Seductive subtlety gives a woman unfathomable power over a man. Be mysterious and let him *slowly* unravel you…remember?

Physical Femininity – Men love it when a woman walks like a woman, talks like a woman, and smells like a woman. This has everything to do with how you present yourself to the outside world in terms of your body. Men love facial expressions and body language that are soft, suggestive, and seductively feminine. Things like submissive eye contact, warm girlish laughter, and a hypnotizing walk are features unique to the female specimen that causes men to respond on a *primal* level. We become helpless when a woman knows how to "strut her stuff."

Feminine Fertility – Because being "sexy" to the opposite sex helps to make babies, illustrating traits of feminine fertility makes a woman more attractive to a man. Radiant skin, physical fitness, and being well groomed all contribute to your "fertility" factors. And the things that make you as different (feminine) as possible from a man (masculine) will pique his interest.

This is why men, though often chided for it, prefer long hair to short. Long, flowing hair makes you different from men (most men at least). This is also why men prefer seeing women in dresses (especially summer dresses) as opposed to pants. A dress makes you appear very different from a man, and different, as we've already agreed on, is good for making babies.

Also keep in mind that quality men prefer a modest display of feminine physical beauty because it communicates that a woman has restraint and has a higher chance of being loyal to one man.

Admiration for all that is Masculine – Masculine men love women who appreciate and adore all that is masculine. Remember, when I say "masculine" I'm not referring essentially to social constructs or cultural stereotypes. I'm referring to *natural masculinity*, or that which makes the men, both intrinsically and outwardly different from women.

Some women just "get it" and they love a man who loves being a man. She lets him be a man, she encourages it, and she cherishes the fact that she's free to be as feminine as she wants because she's with a man, through and through. Admittedly, some women have lost what it means to let a man "be a man", which leads me to the next section…

Let Him Lead…He'll Feel Like THE Man Around You

I know most people say that a good woman can make a man feel like a man when he's around her.

Well, I have the opinion that only a man can make himself "feel" like a man. However, a woman who knows what she's doing can help him by allowing him the opportunity to show just how much of a man he really is.

Men have ginormous egos, and they love to have them stroked by a woman. You can make a man fall in love with you simply by allowing him the pleasure of feeling like he's a big, strong man around you. Believe me, the more a great guy feels like he's "the man" around you, the more he will WANT to be around you.

To this day, I'm still puzzled at how some women have developed the unconscious habit of emasculating the men in their lives and then they always wonder why they end up being alone. If your way of communicating with a man is to bust his balls at every chance you get, you're going to have a hard time keeping any Mr. McDreamy interested in you longer than a few weeks.

It's not rocket science. A man will SEEK OUT the company of a woman who encourages him to be the man and who allows him the gift of feeling masculine around her. Which brings me back to the sentence I keep repeating over and over in each of these chapters: Let him lead.

It's Okay to Play...

Want to know a little secret about men that's so silly you probably won't believe me? Okay, okay...I'll tell you: *We actually enjoy it when a woman plays damsel in distress.* Silly huh? Now, let me explain. Sometimes it's fun to have an opportunity to prove our worth to the women we're interested in or the woman we love. We're naturally hard-wired to *want to impress* a woman. We can't help it.

In fact, guys all over the world are studying the latest pick up artist techniques in order to restrain the side of themselves that make it obvious that they're trying to impress you. Why? Because it's widely known (in the seduction community at least) that women are more attracted to men who learn how to become *indifferent* to a woman's approval.

How does this all intertwine with playing the damsel in distress? The application is simple. If men are working so hard trying NOT to impress you (to win your approval), that means there's something *naturally* built into the male psyche that makes us want to. Women who understand this very strange phenomenon in men are the most seductive women on this earth. They've simply trained themselves to cater to a man's need for the respect and admiration of women. By playing the fun little game of damsel-in-distress with a man, you're giving him an opportunity to impress you with his feats of strength, storehouse of knowledge, or fearlessness.

Let's go back to high school for a moment. Do you remember the girls who really had a way with guys? Barring any slutty behavior, some girls realized early on that the best way to get and keep a young man's attention was to acknowledge his need to impress women. Some girls, the smart ones, took this knowledge with them as they matured and probably enjoy the same sort of success with the opposite sex that they did back in high school.

So what's a girl to do then? How do you make a man feel more like a man around you? Well, since I'm so generous, I'll give you a few simple examples. Try these ideas on for size:

1. Encourage him to make more decisions and ask him his opinion (with the intention of actually listening to him). He'll feel like you respect his wisdom and intelligence.

2. Give him important "manly" jobs like fixing things or removing pests (lizards, frogs, spiders, etc.) from your presence. And compliment him as he does it. You don't have to play helpless, but rather encourage his masculine need to protect and serve by showing him that you need him, and that you enjoy having him around. By giving him the opportunity to do those things for you that you find complicated or dreadful, he'll feel like you respect his desire to serve and protect you.

3. Show off your true womanly nature by making your appearance more feminine. Take care of your physical appearance and try wearing clothing that is soft and delicate. Men love the sight and touch of soft materials on women, and it brings out something primal within them that makes them want to embrace and protect.

The Woman On the Outside Tells Us What's On the Inside

I understand that different men find different things physically attractive about a woman, but all men would agree that women who pay special attention to what their appearance is communicating to men are much more attractive. As I mention in my book, 101 Things

<u>Your Dad Never Told You About Men,</u> paying little attention to your appearance doesn't communicate your own self-approval, self-acceptance, or some other message of female empowerment. The only thing it communicates to a man is "I'm not interested in attracting or keeping a man...thanks!"

The *beautiful* woman is the one who can still wow a man with her loveliness, in both appearance and character. This has little to do with a woman's age or physical measurements, and more to do with the way a woman uses what she already possesses to captivate a man's senses.

How can a girl display the inward character of feminine beauty on the outside? Simple...learn how to fall in love with you. I know, I know, the answer sounds cliché and you've probably heard it in thousands of books and articles about "what men want", but seriously, it's that simple. Self-love will communicate itself by how well you take care of yourself. This is a sure way to keep a guy interested in you for the long-term since men love to be with a woman who makes an effort to be physically irresistible.

True Beauty Lies in a Woman's Behavior

I know how cliché this sounds as well, but a woman's physical beauty is only a part of the attraction game. High-quality men want a lot more than flawless skin, seductive eyes, and a shapely figure. They want substance, the kind of qualities in a woman that can add value to their lives over the long-term. In fact, to a man of high character, physical beauty and even charm are less important than a woman's behavior.

The relationship is inverse, meaning the higher his character (moral fiber, personal beliefs, noble ideals, manly virtue, etc.) the less effect a woman's physical beauty has on him. That's not to say physical beauty has no importance at all (I'd be lying to you if I did), but its significance in attracting and most importantly, keeping a high-quality man is only partial. To a high-quality man, there has to be more to a woman than meets the eye.

The Key to a Woman's Allure

There's a certain aspect about a woman's personality that adds to her feminine grace. It's the secret attribute of the world's most irresistible women; they're the ones who possess a certain *je ne sais quoi* that makes men helplessly drawn to and captivated by them. These women aren't the most gorgeous women out there, neither are they the most brilliant, but they do have one thing in common…they have a tantalizingly girlish, *joie de vivre*. Their love for and effortless enjoyment of life makes them a delight to be around for any man. Women who exude their inner joy tend to project their positivity to those around them. They can become the center of attention without trying, as they laugh, smile, and radiate cheerfulness into the world.

When you can focus on having fun and sharing it, you become far more attractive to the men around you. Read that last sentence again. In the same way "girls just wanna have fun", remember that guys actually want the same thing. For instance, back in my dating days (before I met my beautiful, graceful, adoring wife), I figured out a little attitude shift that resulted in me attracting more wonderful, interesting women to date. It was this: *Every time I went out, no matter what, I committed to having a good time and ensuring that those around me had a good time as well.* Now, this didn't mean I became the life of the party, but it did mean that my "fun" and happiness was not conditional. This meant that I would have fun with my friends, whether or not women danced with us. This meant that I would have fun with my friends, whether or not the music sucked or the venue was dull.

And you know what happened? Every single time I remember making this commitment (and then teaching my friends to do the same), I had a ridiculously good time with my friends AND women were always drawn to us. It's almost as if women realized that my friends and I were a blast to be around and that we weren't "looking" for approval, acceptance, or the attention of women. We were more concerned with having fun and sharing that fun. This attitude made us highly attractive to the opposite sex. When you develop the **habit** of seeing the bright side of things, you tend to get more out of life more often than not.

It's a total drain when the woman you're interested in is constantly unhappy, cynical, pessimistic, or dispassionate. On the other hand (and at the risk of sounding cheesy), it's wonderful when a man can be in the presence of a woman who's completely enamored with and actively engaged in the miracle that is life. There really is something magical (and mysterious) about a woman who can have fun AND share her happiness with others even in the most boring situations and discomforting circumstances.

Not every woman is going to be a Victoria Secret model, and men are OKAY with that, seriously. But finding a cheerful woman is worth more to a man than a fortune. She can uplift his spirits when things don't work out for him as well as share in his victories with unbridled enthusiasm. In fact, the woman who possesses a joy for life has a serious competitive advantage over her peers.

A quality man realizes that a graceful, cheerful spirit is a rare quality to find in a woman, and he'll walk the ends of the earth to keep a woman like this happily committed to him. Why? Because few things petrify a man more than the idea of spending his life with a woman whose happiness (i.e., mood) is completely unpredictable and utterly dependent on conditions.

In short, cheerfulness and optimism are VERY attractive qualities in a woman. Feminine cheerfulness makes a man feel alive, and they make a woman appear mysterious, invaluable, feminine, and touched by God himself. Just like any other characteristic, cheerfulness can be developed. It is quite possible to nurture a joyful spirit.

In his autobiography, steel magnate, Andrew Carnegie once wrote that to him his sunny disposition was worth more than a fortune (possibly his), and that he believed that it could be cultivated by anyone who was willing to try. Learn how to cultivate joy and practice gratitude, because these are some of the keys that lead to a cheerful personality; one that can win the hearts of those high-quality men that other women would consider unattainable.

Chapter 4:

Something He Desperately Craves ...Even More Than Sex...

4

Unconditional Respect

The ONE Thing He Craves...Even More Than Sex

Yes, you read that correctly. When it comes to cultivating a lasting relationship with a great guy, respect is more important than sex. In fact, many husbands out there can attest to the fact that they can function better sexually when they feel respected and admired by their wives. In all honesty, I didn't want to list this quality because I assumed it would be common knowledge to women at this point.

But after some pondering and observation, I realize that a lot of advice out there for women who want to improve how they relate with men either focus on the externals or ways to be manipulative. Things like being sexy and being phenomenal in bed won't mean squat to a high-quality man if your ability to show him respect is critically impaired. It is impossible for a man to fall in love and stay in love with you if he feels as if you do not RESPECT him. Impossible.

Men feel love very differently from women. Where women crave love and affection as their primary relationship needs, men desperately crave respect and admiration. We want to be esteemed highly by the woman we love and we want to feel as if she acknowledges our need for unconditional respect, at least in a long-term relationship. Now, when I say *unconditional respect*, I mean respect that doesn't rely on how you might be feeling about him at the moment or how attractive, wealthy, happy, etc., he is at the moment. If you cannot respect a man when he's down on his luck, you're going to have a problem in your relationship.

What if the roles were reversed? Can you imagine being in a relationship with a man whose love for you is based on a condition? Imagine if you're going through a rough patch in your life and your guy just up and decides that he's not going to love you or show you any affection until you get back on your feet. You would probably call him a selfish pig, a big dumb jerk, or something a bit more colorful.

If so, imagine how a man feels when the woman he loves easily loses respect for him and treats him with contempt the minute life deals him a bad hand. Her respect is conditional and because of that she's unstable and her loyalties are questionable. Granted, men, just like women, are subject to the laws of attraction. Sometimes he's sexier than other times, and that's natural. But what I'm talking about are the unchangeable, which are…love and respect.

He Needs Responsibility

High-quality men understand that one of the most important qualities of being a man is responsibility. I'm sure you can agree with me that one of the most unattractive things is a man who abhors responsibility. Whether it's responsibility for his actions, for his community, his health, family, etc., it doesn't matter. The better the man, the better his ability to accept and manage responsibility. What can be frustrating though is dealing with people who try to undermine your authority, or put another way, question your capacity to be responsible. If you rob a man of his responsibilities, whether your intentions are good or not, you're essentially robbing him of his manhood.

Respect His Needs

To truly respect a man means that you understand his needs…as a MAN. This means that you must take into account the things that are important to his *masculine identity* and esteem him for those things rather than hate or hinder him. Being jealous or unwilling to understand and make room in your life for his deepest needs will make it difficult for you to attract and keep a good man.

Take the whole concept of "guy time" for example. If a man has friends then that's a good thing. You should want him to want to spend time with his buddies on a regular basis. This is a healthy aspect of life for a well-rounded man. This actually ensures that he's not some crazy outcast who is incapable of functioning in normal society.

Some women may actually undervalue the significance of a guy needing time to bond with his buddies. Without this male bonding time, a man could become out of touch with how he relates to other men. He may also lose his manly drive to achieve and conquer, which comes from a healthy support of male friends. He needs his time with the guys, and if you can communicate that you understand that it is a necessity, he will love you even more for it. So keep in mind that there will be things in his life that may be a necessity for him that might not be all that important to you. Recognize these things and esteem him or encourage him in them, assuming of course, that such things will not jeopardize the integrity of your relationship.

Respect All Around

Kind of like the whole "one ring to rule them all" concept from *The Lord of the Rings*, the quality of being *unconditionally respectful* to a man is the one quality that rules them all. I'll even go as far as to say that if you can grasp and apply this one quality, you'll be amazed at how easy developing the other qualities can be.

For example, when you're honest with a man, you're respecting his intelligence and his principles. You're showing him that you respect him (and yourself) enough to be truthful with him. Even more so, it shows him that you're a woman of principles, and if you didn't know by now, good men love women that act based on her principles as opposed to how she feels or what she wants.

Another example - when you're supportive and encourage him to pursue his dreams, you're respecting his ideals and goals, the very things that drive him in life. When you allow him to feel like a man around you (remember the whole damsel-in-distress bit) you're respecting his need to play his role as a protector and provider for the woman he loves. Also, when you're not interested in trying to change him to suit your needs, he feels as if you respect his personal identity, his desire for independence, and his right to be loved for who he is as he is.

This kind of respect even flows into other areas like having respect for his friends and his family. I should mention that aside from disrespecting him in front of others, the fastest way to turn a man off is to disrespect those who he holds dearest to him. You'll notice that even among other men, honor and loyalty are non-negotiable in a healthy male friendship. Aside from harmless jokes between buddies, any sign of blatant disrespect is not tolerated, especially among high-quality men. Seriously, it's that important to a man.

Easy to Love, Hard to Respect

Have you ever thought about why men pursue women with standards for long-term relationships and marriage? Have you ever considered why it's much harder for a husband to forgive his wife if she has an affair than it is for a wife to forgive her husband? Have you ever thought about why guys, in their male friendships, live by a certain code of honor? The answer is simple: It's because men are naturally designed to speak the language of respect.

Whether it's built in genetically or it's more of a social construct doesn't matter, the fact remains that men have an easier time being respectful to each other AND women. Women, in comparison to men, have much more difficulties when it comes to showing respect. If we consider the whole love and respect concept, we can agree that women, by nature and generally speaking, have an easier time displaying acts of love and giving affection both in how they relate to each other and with men. Men on the other hand aren't as quick to display their love and affection, at least when compared to women. With this in mind, we can conclude that a man can just as easily remove his love from a disrespectful woman as a woman can remove her respect from an unloving man.

This is why it is so important for a woman to make a conscious attempt to show a man unconditional respect. It's something that doesn't come *naturally* to her unless she was trained to do so. Now before you throw stones at me, let me explain…

On Daddy Issues

When I say "trained" I mean in a parental sense, and this applies for both men and women. The problem usually starts somewhere in the home where a lack (or poor example) of a father figure has left many men and women confused and even unable to function correctly in their adult relationships. In fact, the popular term for this is called, "daddy issues." If a woman isn't brought up in a home where her father provided a deep sense of security, she has a higher chance of growing up with a greater distrust in men.

I hate to generalize, but my experiences with the opposite sex have yet to prove me wrong. It's much easier to cultivate a relationship with a woman who either has a good relationship with her father (or some father figure) or who found a way to deal with her daddy issues. The MAIN reason for this is because women that have good relationships with their dads usually have higher self-esteem and therefore, are more respectful to men.

Therefore, if you find yourself having overwhelming challenges when it comes to trusting and respecting men, don't hesitate to seek out help whether professionally or from a few great books. You don't have to suffer in your adult relationships because of your past. There are more than enough resources available out there to help you overcome your insecurities.

I Don't Think I Can Respect Him

Remember, men feel love when they know they're respected. If you're finding it difficult to respect a man, then chances are he may not be the right guy in the first place. If you can't respect him as a man, you won't be able to love him completely as a woman. You may have loving feelings toward him and you may enjoy receiving his affections, but if you cannot reciprocate that love with unconditional respect, you're robbing him of the opportunity to find a woman that can. Besides, if you have difficulty respecting him, you're better off with a man that makes it easier for you to just let him lead. Think about it.

Chapter 5:

Here's the Trait That Makes Him Open Up to You...

5

Understanding (Complete Acceptance):

Be the Woman That Can Love the Ugly Things About Him

I'm sure I don't have to go into too much detail with this one do I? No man wants to end up being with a woman whose sole mission is to shape and mold him into the kind of man she really wants. In fact, if you have to shape and mold a man into the kind of man you want, here is a tip for you…he's not the right guy!

I know some women might have some experience in transforming a man into her ideal, but I can guarantee you that no self-respecting man who exudes confidence and authority is going to allow a woman to change him into what she wants. A woman who does succeed in changing a man to fit her ideal usually ends up with a resentful empty shell of a man who's mastered the art of sacrificing his self-respect just to keep her happy. Either that or she ends up with something else as equally unsatisfying: perpetual singleness. I repeat, a self-respecting man will not stand being manipulated by ANY woman; no matter how gorgeous or charming she appears.

If you want to make a high-quality man fall in love

with you then you need to learn how to just let him be himself. A good man won't try to change you. If you're the right woman for him, he will accept you as you are, flaws and all, and he won't make it his life's mission to make you into the kind of woman that he wants.

Trying to change a man to fit your ideal is always…in every situation…a bad idea. Trying to change someone into what YOU want or what you think they should be will only lead to anger and disappointment. The more a man can truly be himself around you without feeling like you'll try to change him, the more comfortable he will become around you which will then make it easier for him to commit to you in the long-run.

If a great guy feels as if he's being manipulated into doing or becoming something he's not just to make you happy, it'll be impossible for him to fall in love with you. If he's a quality guy, he has his own sense of independence that he doesn't want to just give up because of a woman. You're going to have to learn how to be patient and understanding with him and give him the space he needs to make mistakes, to make you unhappy from time-to-time, and to get on your last nerve.

Finding your Prince Charming isn't anything like a Disney animated film. No matter how perfect you think he is, your Mr. McDreamy WILL do things that upset you. If you find that you're always tempted to pull out your fix-a-man toolkit while dating a particular guy, chances are, he's not the right guy for you. Just because you think he's not living up to his potential doesn't mean that some other lucky girl won't think so. It's up to him to decide what he's capable of and act on that awareness. As I've already repeated a thousand times already: let him lead.

If it Bothers You Now...

If it bothers you now it will definitely bother you later. Don't make the false assumption that his impaired sense of fashion or negligent grooming habits is going to improve in the future. Don't make the even worse assumption of thinking that you'll be the catalyst to make him want to change these things in the future. Some women have this idea that if they're the ones to change a man, they're the winners. They think: "If I can change him that must mean that he loves me the most. I'm his best…I'm special!"

You can save yourself from a ton of frustrating relationships with men if you obliterate this belief from your mind immediately. This sort of thinking is based on how women *think* men are instead of how we actually behave. In fact, the ugly truth is quite contrary to this belief. The more you try to change something about him that he's not actively interested in changing himself, the worse he'll think of you.

If you start off changing little things about a man here and there you'll find it difficult to stop. Every little thing that annoys you about him will become your personal little project and you'll soon go out of your way to find things you can improve upon. Things can get even worse when you start comparing your "man-project" to your friends' boyfriends and husbands. You'll want to make competitive upgrades to your man-project just to ensure that he's better than the competition. I know this all sounds ridiculous, but believe me, it happens. This is not a fun road to travel down, especially for the man who's getting worked on.

Now, it's not wrong to encourage him to grow and to help him get where he'd like to be in life, but this has to be for HIS benefit first and foremost, not yours. A good man can judge a situation objectively and he'll discern the motives behind your "let me fix you" behaviors. If your intentions are sincere, he'll see you more as a godsend and an irreplaceable helpmate that has his best interest at heart. If your behavior in this area stem from self-interest, he might begin to resent your meddlesome attempts to change him.

Learn to influence him without intruding on his self-identity. When a man is influenced, he'll seek change on his own even if you were the catalyst for it. If he feels as if your attempts are intrusive however, he's going to become obstinate and unwilling to change, even if it's for his own good.

Subtle Signs of Disrespect

Personal transformation is very difficult, especially if a habit or way of thinking has taken a lifetime to develop. The main problem with a woman trying to change a man is how that man generally perceives it. Where you may be thinking, "I only want what's best for him", he's thinking, "She's acting like my mother." The whole act of trying to change a man is an indirect insult to his ego. It communicates to him that you're not happy with him and that you'll do whatever you can to change him to make yourself happy.

The main problem with a woman trying to change a man is twofold. One, he'll feel as if the man he is now is insufficient to make you happy, which over time can undermine his self-image and cripple his self-confidence. And two, you come off as manipulative, selfish, and nagging, as opposed to being helpful, compassionate, and proactive – the things you thought you were. A man with a healthy amount of self-respect won't subject himself to this kind of perceived abuse for long. Instead of giving you enough time to cripple his self-confidence or nag him to death, he'll leave. The whole thing is a matter of respect. And only by fully accepting a man, flaws and all, will he feel respected and therefore, loved.

When He Doesn't Mind Your Influence

There will be some instances where a man has no qualms about letting you "upgrade" a certain part of his life, especially if he knows that your input is invaluable and will make him a better man. For example, the guy you're dating might not mind the little tweaks you make to his wardrobe or the gradual adjustments you make to some other area of his life. This doesn't necessarily mean that he lacks self-respect. Some men understand the value of a good woman's input, especially when he *feels* as if her input comes from a place of deep respect (there's that word again) for him rather than her own self-interest.

A quality man realizes that the *influence* (not manipulation) of the right woman can help him reach his fullest potential and get ahead in life. However, he has to come to this realization on his own. In the same way you need time to appraise his value to you, a man needs time to appraise your value to him. Trying to coerce him into allowing you to improve some area of his life is a sure recipe for disaster. Only when he feels that you already accept him the way he is, that you have his best interest at heart, and that your concern for him comes from a place of sincerity will he be open to your influence.

It's not up to you to take responsibility for some area of his life unless he grants you influential access. When you're in a relationship with a man, think of him as the captain and you're his first mate. The first mate only takes the initiative on matters that the captain has already delegated to her. If he doesn't want to delegate his fashion sense or choice of friends to you, leave it alone. While it's natural for a woman to want to "improve" her man, it's only endearing when he doesn't mind her influence in that area.

What if He Does Something Unacceptable?

Excellent question, my dear! If you're dating a man who has behaviors, interests, or beliefs that you find absolutely unacceptable…call the whole thing off. I'm very serious. Once again, this advice sounds like common sense, but after you've become emotionally involved with a great guy you may unconsciously overlook some of his perceived flaws that will get under your skin later on. I stand by my belief that if you find it extremely difficult to accept a man the way he is, it's better off not to continue the relationship.

After the initial romantic attraction wears off and you get a good look at what's under Mr. McDreamy's hood (his insecurities, bad habits, unrefined behaviors, etc.), you must always ask yourself if you can live happily with what you see. If whatever you find under that hood makes you unhappy, fearful, or downright frustrated far too often, do yourself a favor and find someone you won't feel extremely challenged to accept or compelled to change.

But I Don't Want Some Other Guy

I was reluctant to include this section because I KNOW most women, when they *think* they've found a great guy…don't want to let him go. Okay, so admittedly life is a lot more complicated than just "break up with him." Sometimes you're in a situation where you'd rather work things out because you've been together so long. Maybe you're in a situation where you both have a child together. I understand, and if you're experiencing a situation like this, my advice is to try to communicate with your man the best you can.

While it's true that it's a lot easier to find the right guy than to try and change a guy into Mr. Right, it is possible to *influence* a man so that he modifies his behavior to make you happy. In all honesty, this is a topic that's beyond the scope of this book. Asserting your needs to a man in a respectful way and defending your personal boundaries are vital to cultivating a healthy relationship. These are subjects I talk about in my book, Make Him BEG For Your Attention.

If you can't summon up the courage to break up with a man who consistently frustrates you, ignores your needs, and oversteps your personal boundaries, prepare for the very, very difficult challenge of trying to influence him to change. Obviously it's not impossible for people in relationships to change in order to meet each other's needs otherwise ALL marriages would fail. However, do keep in mind that I'm not talking about marriage. I'm talking about dating. And while you're dating a man, remember that you do have OPTIONS. You can try to work things out with a man you absolutely love, but just remember at the end of the day...men don't want to be manipulated into becoming something they're not, no matter how good your intentions are.

Chapter 6:

The One Thing Every Man Desperately Needs From His Woman...

6

Unwavering Loyalty

Be the One Woman He Can Count On...No Matter What

Kings would often go great lengths to ensure that those who serve under them were unwaveringly loyal to them and the kingdom. Without loyalty, a king's rule was subject to all sorts of treachery, and the kingdom would eventually become unstable. If his right hand man lacked complete devotion, the king would be an ineffective ruler.

When it comes to relating to a high-quality man, consider the premise that men like this consider themselves kings. No, they may not have a kingdom, castle or crown, but in terms of how he views himself he believes that he's the kind of man worthy of a woman's true devotion. Why? Because in most cases, a man like this is more than willing to do the same for a good woman. In short, a good man wants unwavering loyalty from the woman he loves, end of story.

Let's face it; the world can be a sinister place at times. There's no denying it. A man shouldn't feel that way about his own home or in his relationship. A man should feel completely comfortable and at peace with his woman. I'm not saying that things will always be perfect, but rather, more often than not, your boyfriend or husband shouldn't have any doubt in the back of his mind that you might commit treason against him.

Imagine how it feels for a man when the woman he loves betrays him in some way, shape, or form. The betrayal doesn't always have to come in the form of sexual infidelity; it can present itself in the way of dishonesty, slander, and even sabotage. Being disloyal to a man is doing anything that betrays his *confidence* in you. When you speak or act in a way that causes a man to lose confidence in you, you're slowly but surely making yourself *less* desirable and even *less* useful to him. Read that last sentence again.

Some women fail to recognize this simple difference from a high-quality man and the average Joe. Quality men regularly *appraise* the people, places, and things in their life in order to assess whom, how, and what they should devote their time and energy to. The average Joe on the other hand, simply accepts what comes his way without a second thought. Consistent betrayal of a quality man's confidence results in a decrease in your value, at least to him. I'm not saying you have to be perfect, because that's just ridiculous. But keep in mind that men like this do have higher standards, with relationship faithfulness being one of them.

Confidence Keeps Him Open

Some women complain that the men in their lives don't seem to "open up" to them. Truthfully, if you want your man to "open up" to you and show you more of his "softer" side, then you must communicate to him that you are here to serve (love) him unconditionally, and *only him*. Show him that you won't ever take advantage of him when he's down on his luck or vulnerable. This point can't be stressed enough. The more a man can feel completely safe and open with his woman, the more he will trust, depend, and serve her, as a good man should.

He wants to know without a shadow of a doubt that he can place his confidence in you and that he can put his all into the relationship. Of course, I assume you already know that you shouldn't lie to him, cheat on him, or steal from him. These things go without saying. But here's a few more that many women seem to overlook:

1. You must refuse to be petty and malicious to him, especially when he's down.

2. Refuse to complain negatively about him to your friends, family, and co-workers.

3. Never insult him or downplay his importance to others, especially his children.

4. Keep your issues and arguments private, unless of course it's professional help.

5. Resolve your issues as quickly as possible, and never go to bed angry.

6. Be open and honest with one another and learn to have the most stress free relationship possible.

Every man sees himself as a king in his home and relationship, as every woman should see herself as a confident and capable queen. Make your man feel like a king by communicating your loyalty to him. Encourage his masculine spirit and he'll continuously serve you in strength and dignity.

How to Prove Your Loyalty

Think of cultivating a relationship with a man like getting into a business partnership. Like a business, the relationship itself is an entity that greatly affects both parties involved. Any sort of disloyal behavior that threatens the health of the business also threatens the livelihood of those involved. A man wants to rest assured on the knowledge that his woman is loyal by *nature*. He doesn't want to end up with a woman who has to consistently struggle to maintain her loyalty to him. And because of that, a wise man will consciously be on the lookout for any behaviors that either illustrates your capacity for loyalty or betrayal.

In short, in the same way a man will have to prove to you that he's worth your time and attention (assuming you see yourself as a prize catch), you're going to have to prove to him that cultivating a relationship with you will not cause him harm in the long run.

Remember, men want women that are *loyal by nature*. This means that, just like every other irresistible quality in this book, showing absolute loyalty to the man you're in a relationship with should become a part of your character. But how do men "test" a woman's loyalty? And how can a great gal such as yourself develop this characteristic and display it to a man? Both are excellent questions.

First of all, while dating you, a man may curiously ask you on a whim if you'd still be with him if he wasn't handsome, successful, had social status, came from a good family, etc. Questions like this hint to a man's need to know if you're going to stick around even if some essential aspect of his masculine identity begins to fade with time or circumstance. In short, he wants to know for sure that you're in it for the long-haul and that you're not going to bail on him the minute he loses his hair, gets fired from his high-paying job, contracts a debilitating sickness etc. Men need reassurance too, because few things are worse than building a life with a woman who's only in it when things are going smoothly. Men want loyalty.

Now, a smart woman understands this deep need and she'll do whatever she can to build the confidence he has in her. Here's the secret: *Show him, in subtle or not so subtle ways that you're with him because of the man he is. Make him feel reassured that it's his character that you're attracted to the most, and not the external things about him.* Here are a few ways to make this happen:

1. Reassure Him that He's Not a Category to You

Yes, men like to feel that they're irreplaceable just as much as women do. If a man starts to feel as if you chose to be with him because he fits neatly within some category of yours, commitment phobia will hit him like a ton of bricks. It's a gut feeling a man gets when he senses that he's *not* your "big picture." Instead, your "big picture" is: married with kids, high earning husband, arm candy for life, a good father, boyfriend with his own business, future doctor, knight-in-shining armor, etc., etc.

Men, quality men, aren't simpletons. We understand that a woman wants these things, and that's fine, but if we begin to feel that a woman wants these things *more* than the man that's attached to such things there's going to be a serious problem. Don't make him feel as if he's interchangeable with some other guy.

Now, I'm a very practical guy, and I don't insist that women waste their time dating guys who cannot fulfill their relationship needs. If you want marriage someday and he doesn't, then that's a conflict of interest and there's nothing wrong with moving on. However, if you're always more *obsessed* with what a man can do for you as opposed to creating a lasting, intimate connection with him, chances are you might chase a lot of good men away because they didn't feel that your interest in them was genuine. Don't make him feel like a category.

2. Appreciate the Qualities that Got Him Where He is

Some women have both the gift and the curse of meeting a man when he already has a high level of success. The gift is that he's dealt with a lot of his inner issues that used to hold him back from success and happiness, so now you don't have to deal with it. The curse is that he's incurred a new set of inner issues that might hold him back from trusting a woman, so now you have an interesting challenge on your hand.

Obviously this isn't a hard and fast rule, but naturally, the more successful a man becomes in the socioeconomic arena, the more prudence he has to exercise when choosing his relationships. It's easy to be loved and adored by women when you're on top of your game; too easy. The challenge for a man is figuring out when a woman truly loves HIM as opposed to the success that's already attached to him. I've already discussed the importance of being supportive in another chapter, so that applies here as well.

Aside from playing the role of a supportive first mate, the other key to convincing a man of your loyalty is through the way you appreciate him. Yes, it's that simple. Now, let's say that the man you're dating is highly successful and is already doing well for himself. And let's also assume that you really do love him for who he is as opposed to what he's attained. What you must do then is emphasize the qualities of character that got him where he is.

If he's spent the last five to ten years of his life climbing the corporate ladder, and he's proud of it, praise his persistence and his diligence. If he's built up a successful software company while working two jobs, praise his tenacity, industrious habits, and work ethic. Even outside of the socioeconomic arena, a man can have insecurities about his success when relating with the women who want him. For example, if he's a stellar med student, praise his manly resilience and resolve. On the other hand, if he's an up and coming sports star, praise his high level of self-discipline.

Successful men want to be appreciated for being self-made success stories. That's not to say that all they want is praise and adulation, but when a man is recognized for overcoming weaknesses and overwhelming circumstances he'll feel that you just "get him", so to speak. So learn to appreciate a man's struggles and fall in love with the qualities of character he's developed because of it. It's a vital key to earning the trust of an already successful man.

3. Empathize with His Challenges…Even if You Can't Relate

No matter where your Mr. McDreamy is in life, he's going to experience insecurities and external challenges that you will not be able to relate to for various reasons. Let's take our previous example of an already highly successful man. Let's say he has just completed a business deal that nets him more money in a month than you make in a year, but that during the deal, he had a falling out with his business partner. He's hurt because he feels taken advantage of by his partner, even though he's just made a truckload of money. Now, some women won't be able to comprehend the challenge. You know for sure that the deal has made him more financially abundant, but you can't understand why he'd be upset over the deal.

It may seem illogical at first, but keep in mind that men have feelings too, regardless of how much outward success they possess. If he feels hurt and manipulated by his business partner, you have an opportunity to show him sympathy and understanding. Successful or not, a man is still a man, and he wants a loyal woman who stands by his side when he's happy or hurting.

Another way you can display empathy to him is by being empathetic with others. If you can empathize with others, no matter what their position is in life, a man is more likely to trust you. Granted, we can't give everyone around us the same level of love and attention, but we can give them our respect. If you treat people differently based on their external success or lack thereof, you may just treat your Mr. McDreamy the same way. If you habitually turn your back on people the minute they slip up, your guy may feel that you might do the same to him. Your loyalty will be in constant question in his mind.

Treat everyone you come into contact with as equals. If a street beggar and your favorite celebrity said something disrespectful to you, how differently would you respond to each of them? Give it some thought.

How Demonstrations of Loyalty Can Land You a Boyfriend

If you're getting to know Mr. McDreamy and he's obviously showing signs that he's seriously interested in an exclusive relationship with you, the first thing you should do is be honest. Let's say you're still "seeing" your ex (for whatever reason) and Mr. McDreamy wants you to be his girlfriend. If he doesn't ask you about your ex, just do the next best thing and stop seeing the guy.

Actually, the other guy (or guys) doesn't even have to be your ex. If you're casually dating other guys but Mr. McDreamy seems to be the best candidate…get rid of the other suitors immediately. And if he asks you if you're seeing anyone else, be honest with him but also let him know your intentions. When a man wants an exclusive relationship, he doesn't want any doubts in his mind in regards to your loyalty.

For instance, if he asks you if you're dating other guys, tell him that you are but that you're looking for something more. Don't lie. Some guys, the wiser, more cunning ones, will choose to keep things casual with you until YOU take the initiative to stop seeing other men. He won't tell you that he's waiting for you to drop the other guys outright, but trust me…that's his game. It's a pretty ingenious way to: 1. Test a woman's interest level, and 2. Determine her loyalty factor. When you do stop seeing other men and subtly communicate this new development to him, chances are he'll be more than thrilled to make you his girlfriend.

How Quality Men Play the Waiting Game

I thought I should mention here that a great guy isn't going to try and pressure you into being loyal to him. This is absurd behavior and it's actually a bit obsessive. In my humble opinion, if I had to strong-arm a woman into being faithful to me, that means that I'm either not being the man I'm suppose to be or she wasn't the right quality of woman to begin with. As a man gets to know you, he's not going to expect you to just drop everything and everyone else for his sake. Trust takes time to build, and as a relationship naturally develops, so should the expectation of unwavering loyalty.

Men who understand how to play the dating game understand that acting counter-intuitively gets them better results. For instance, I'm sure you can agree with me that you'll lose interest in a man who immediately demands that you treat him with respect and that you remain absolutely loyal to him, even though you've only been dating him for a week or two. It speaks volumes about his insecurities, and his strong-arming will make you feel like your freedom of choice is being stifled.

A smart man is going to allow YOU to display your level of loyalty to him. In fact, he won't push you or demand anything. He'll wait patiently for you to recognize his value and acknowledge your level of interest by how eager you are to get rid of other suitors in order to make room for an exclusive relationship with him.

A high-quality man approaches dating with an abundance mentality. He can just as easily walk away from you if you're incapable of recognizing that he's worth your all. Once again, this isn't a hard and fast rule, but high-quality men are excellent judges of character. In short, they date to win, and what they want to win is a great girlfriend, and perhaps even a potential wife.

Serial Flirters, Attention Seekers, and the Low Self-Esteemed

Disloyalty can show its ugly face in many subtle or not-so-subtle ways. One of them is flirting with other men. It really doesn't matter if you consider yourself a natural flirt and believe "that's just who I am." It's both disrespectful to the man you want to cultivate a relationship with and it weakens his trust in you. I mention flirting because it can lead to other kinds of disloyal behavior, i.e. cheating.

Naturally, I understand some women need to be seen as attractive and desirable by the opposite sex. Men have this same need as well, but the problem for both sexes arises when this need isn't kept in check. If you find yourself craving the attention of other men, even when you're already in a relationship, there's a chance that you may have self-esteem issues. This isn't a hard and fast rule, especially if the man you're with doesn't pay you any attention. But I'm sure you can agree with me that constantly needing attention from men can become a problem.

This sort of behavior is driven by a woman's need to have her ego stroked. When a man who is not her own gives her attention, it reaffirms her of her desirability and attractiveness. Experienced men have a much easier time discerning when a woman is perpetually starving for the attention of men. They may not see it at first, but you can't hide what's inside. If a good man begins to see signs that a woman is more preoccupied with getting the attention of new men as opposed to appreciating the man she already has, he'll quickly realize that she might not be the right girl after all.

Chapter 7:

An Attribute That Keeps Him Loyal (A Woman's Secret Weapon)...

7

Proactive Love

The Power of an Unselfish, Affectionate Woman

A proactive lover is simply someone who understands the needs and desires of their significant other and goes out of their way to ensure that these needs and desires are met. If you want to make a man feel like a king, then learn to become a proactive lover. And if you want to escalate your relationship with a man on a more emotional level, being a proactive lover is the surefire way to ensure that he gets the message (remember: be seductively subtle).

Give Him What He Needs

One of the keys to being a proactive lover lies in how effective you are at understanding the way the man you're interested in prefers to receive love. For example, some men need more words of affirmation to feel loved, while others need acts of service. Some guys need more physical affection. Others require small thoughtful gifts, and some even require more quality time to feel special to a woman.

This subject is also covered much more in-depth in bestselling author, Gary Chapman's book, <u>The Five</u>

Love Languages. In it, he defines the five love languages and how important it is for couples to communicate in the love language that their significant other desperately needs. Here's a short summary of the different love languages and how a man needs to be loved:

1. Words of Affirmation

This love language uses words as the primary way of expressing love. And when a man's main love language is words of affirmation he needs to constantly be affirmed of the way you feel about him and how much you appreciate the man he is and the things he's done. This is his primary way of feeling love.

Phrases such as, "Babe, you look especially handsome in that blue suit" or "I feel like the most beautiful woman in the world when I'm with you" will make him feel adored by you. Let him know when he astounds you, and be as sincere with your approbations as you can. Be sure to let him know just how much you admire his external and internal strengths as well, and tell him when you're proud of his accomplishments, both big and small. Men like this need lots of verbal encouragement. This doesn't make him weak, but it gives you an opportunity to fill a need that only a loving woman can.

2. Acts of Service

If a man's love language is acts of service, to him, your actions will always speak louder than your words. Verbally expressing your admiration and love for him might only get you so far. Instead, men like this require action. A man who gives and receives love through acts of service might go to the ends of the earth to serve you, but he'll expect reciprocation.

Cultivating a relationship with men who need acts of service means doing things for him that show him how much you care. The benefit of this love language is that you don't have to guess what his needs are. All you have to do is ask him. Ask him about the things you can do for him to make him happy and follow through on those things (assuming they're reasonable of course). The more you take initiative in this department the more desired he would feel by you.

3. Receiving Gifts

When a man's love language is receiving gifts it means that a token of your appreciation will make him feel deeply loved by you. When you go out of your way to purchase, create, or obtain something unique and tangible for him, he might think to himself, "She gave me this wonderful gift for no reason, she must have been thinking about me!"

Now, just because a man may love receiving gifts, it does not make him high maintenance. When a man prefers receiving special gifts as a sign of love he usually only wants something tangible that reminds him of your thoughtfulness and appreciation.

Most of the time, men prefer special gifts that are very practical in nature, something they can use on a daily basis or in specific situations. On the other hand, some men might prefer gifts that are a lot more sentimental. A guy like this is sometimes more romantic in nature, and he might easily become putty in the hands of a woman who knows what special surprise will put a smile on his face.

4. Quality Time

When a man's primary love language is quality time, it means that when you're spending time with him he wants your full, undivided attention. I'm the type of guy that loves sharing his knowledge with others (sort of like a teacher I guess), and I think on some level I crave an audience every now and then. Because of this, I tend to crave quality time. I don't need a lot of time, but when I do...I want all the attention I can get. I love it when my beloved spends that time with me and lets me go on and on about something new I've just learned or something I'm passionate about. And vice versa, when I'm spending quality time with her I ensure that she has my full, undivided attention. No distractions, no daydreaming, just her and me.

When a man wants quality time, he wants you to be fully engaged with him. He doesn't want you to have that look on your face that you'd rather be doing something else. He also doesn't want to compete with your cell phone, laptop, or lap dog even. He just wants you and all of you, for the time you're together. He wants to feel as if it's only you and him, alone in a private space that you both own and possess in its entirety. He wants to have an experience with you that feels effortless and calming. And it's interactions like this that melts his troubles away and makes it easy for him to fall in love with you again and again. In short, guys who love quality time want to feel as if he's the most important thing in your entire world, at least for a while.

5. Physical Touch

When a man's primary love language is physical touch it simply means that the right and appropriate touch will make him feel appreciated and desirable. He wants to literally feel you express how much you care for him by the kind of physical contact he finds both emotionally satisfying and pleasurable. The tricky thing about physical touch is that it will vary from man to man, as well as from culture to culture. It's important to understand just what kinds of physical contact will make your Mr. McDreamy feel loved on a deep emotional level.

Making a special effort to hold his hand as you walk together is a great example of this. Even caressing him arm tenderly as you talk to him might also tickle his fancy. Men like this especially need a woman's soft touch to convey her affection. It's guys like this who also have a higher appreciation for giving and receiving back rubs and even cuddling. They want to be touched by a woman, often, and without having to coax her into doing it. They simply want to be touched in the right way that says to them, "Hey, I just love being near to you and I want you as close to me as possible."

Of course, these five, short descriptions are just the tip of the iceberg, but they're enough to get you thinking in the right direction. The Five Love Languages is an extremely popular book, and you may want to look into it to get an enlightened perspective on how you prefer showing and receiving love in comparison with the man you're dating (or hope to date someday).

On Becoming a Proactive Person

To be a proactive lover, you'll have to become a proactive person on the whole. Now, I have to admit that if you're not already a proactive person, developing this particular quality will challenge you, but it has the ability to transform your life for the better. Proactive people make things happen instead of waiting for things to happen. They see life in terms of what they can control and what's out of their control and they focus all of their energy on the former group instead of the latter. Proactive people, more often than not, have a more positive outlook on life and experience greater amounts of success because they spend their energy effectively. In short, proactive people see the world, and therefore their relationships as a source of abundance.

Reactive people focus on what's out of their control and end up burning all of their energy reacting to or worrying about situations that are beyond their ability to change. They experience more negativity as their experiences reaffirm their belief that "things are always out of their control." Reactive people blame everyone and everything around them, whether consciously or subconsciously, for their personal problems. They see the world and their relationships as a source of scarcity.

Love in Action – Treat Him Like a King

I expect that most women understand the importance of supporting a man's passions, but just in case, I'll provide a few examples of proactive love. For starters, let's say for instance that you're dating a guy who loves football. It's important that you understand his passion for the sport and do what's necessary to support his interest. Now, if you don't like football, you simply don't have to like it. You don't have to feign an interest in the sport just to make him fall madly in love with you. However, simple gestures like making sure he doesn't miss his favorite teams, buying him tickets, or even serving him and his buddies some food while they watch the game won't go unnoticed. By being the woman that enhances the quality of his past times and interests, you make yourself an irreplaceable part of his life. It's habitual gestures like this that compel a man to think, "I can't imagine what I'd do without her."

On the other hand, let's say that your man works at a job that you know is stressful. If this is the case, it's important that you play an *active* role to ensure that his time away from work (specifically when he's with you) is pleasant, peaceful, and free from unnecessary conflict. If he comes to visit you straight from work, try having his favorite drink ready for him and maybe even have his favorite music playing in the background to help him relax. You could even try learning how to massage to help him release his tensions.

If the guy you're dating travels a lot or works a potentially dangerous profession, it's a good idea to ensure that the moments he spends with you are memorable and beautiful. Do thoughtful things to ensure that the memories he has of you are vivid and reaffirming. You never know what kinds of temptation he may face on the road if he travels a lot, or what kind of life threatening situations he'll have to overcome if he has a dangerous profession. Many soldiers have confessed that it was the cherished memories of their significant others that helped them to make it back alive to their homes and families.

Granted, these are all general examples, but if you

treat your man like a king he'll be more likely to return to you. Of course, there should always be some sort of balance in everything, and it's up to you to know how much love and nurturing your man needs. Remember, it's not about giving him everything he asks for; it's about catering to those needs that he may neglect to mention. Giving too much of your thought, time, and energy to an unappreciative man will wear you down over time. So with that in mind, never be shy to give, but always respect your own personal boundaries. If you're dating a man who is uninterested in being a proactive lover to you as well, there's a mismatch and it might be time for you to find a man who will reciprocate.

Appreciate Him...A LOT

A man wants to feel that he makes a difference in the world, but specifically, in the world of his woman. You've watched the movies and read the books, and you've seen how a woman who deeply appreciates a man both for his character and his achievements usually accompanies these male heroes.

Many women these days cannot comprehend the importance of simply allowing a man to be a man. What this means is that men have egos, usually large ones. There's no getting around this fact. The women that understand this simple idea are usually the most successful with men, since they also learn how to carefully cater to their egos.

A man must feel that his presence matters to the woman he loves. This doesn't mean that you need to boost his self-esteem, since a great guy should be confident in himself already. However, showing more appreciation for his strengths rather than chastising him for his shortcomings will have a much greater and more positive effect on your relationship in the long run.

Intimacy Escalation

Men sometimes won't know just how much you mean to him (or how bad you want him) if you fail to escalate intimacy. Most men these days, even quality men, aren't able to initiate emotional intimacy by themselves in a relationship. For a man, any sort of escalation in the relationship usually revolves around physical intimacy, which isn't necessarily the same thing as emotional intimacy. Depending on his stance, he's going to want to initiate some sort of physical relationship with you, as soon as possible. So where you may be looking for more emotional intimacy in order to feel confident of his commitment to you, he's going to be looking for physical intimacy in order to feel confident of your commitment to him.

Instinctually, men know that once a woman becomes physically involved, she has a higher chance of being "hooked" on him…for good. If you're not ready for higher levels of physical intimacy, ensure that he understands your stance and respects it. But you're also going to have to take things a bit further than just telling him "no", "not yet", or "not until marriage."

If you want to get what you want from him first (emotional intimacy), you're going to have to be a bit more proactive about what you want. You must be the one to take things to the next level, emotionally. When a man is deeply invested in a woman emotionally, the decision to keep her in his life and sacrifice a chance to be with other women (sexual diversity) becomes a no brainer. You may have a hard time believing this, but in the "game" of love, men are ridiculously outmatched. You, as a woman, have the power to deepen a man's emotional investment and get the love and commitment you want.

But how does a woman escalate the emotional intimacy in a relationship? Well, it's all about getting to know what a man needs and then fulfilling those needs that only YOU, a woman like you, can fulfill. It's your simple gestures of love, loyalty, and desire that will soften his heart and win him over…for good. This is why I saved this quality for last because being a proactive lover is the *habitual application* of the other qualities and points I've already discussed in this book.

Be honest and vulnerable with him. Support him in the way only a woman can. Be unapologetically feminine around him. Show him unconditional respect. Accept him as he is, now, in the present. And illustrate your loyalty to him. The act of doing these things in the language of love he understands will pluck at his masculine heartstrings and make his heart melt. I've seen it happen to men all around me and I've witnessed it happen to me.

The right woman is that one woman who can make us *want* to commit to her. She's the woman that just "gets us" and by being seductively subtle, she can make even the most unattainable man fall in love with her. There's no one trick or tactic that will escalate things with a man on an emotional level. It's the thoughtfulness and significance of your acts of love that will win him over. Guaranteed.

About Bruce Bryans

Bruce is a successful author who's written various best-selling books for men and women who want to improve the quality of their relationships. He's also written many articles for various online publications and enjoys sharing the triumphs (and failures) of his love life with anyone who enjoys a good laugh or a life lesson.

When he isn't tucked away in some corner of his house writing a literary masterpiece (or so he thinks), Bruce spends most of his time engaged in his hobbies or being a romantic nuisance to the love of his life. And after spending most of his twenties studying books about psychology, seduction, dating, and relationships, he's happy to finally have a gorgeous, exotic, sun-kissed goddess with a heart of gold to share his life with.

Most Recommended Books by Bruce Bryans:

Here's the web address to my book list where you can access all of the books listed:

http://www.amazon.com/author/brucebryans

101 Things Your Dad Never Told You About Men: The Good, Bad, And Ugly Things Men Want And Think About Women And Relationships

In 101 Things Your Dad Never Told You About Men, you'll learn what high-quality men want from women and what they think about love, sex, and romance. You'll learn how to seduce the man you want or captivate the man you love because you'll know exactly what makes him tick.

Make Him BEG For Your Attention: 75 Communication Secrets For Captivating Men And Getting The Love And Commitment You Deserve

In Make Him BEG For Your Attention, you'll discover how to talk to a man so that he listens to you, opens up to you, and gives you what you want without a fuss.

Send Him A Signal: 61 Secrets For Indicating Interest And Attracting The Attention Of Higher Quality Men

In Send Him A Signal, you'll learn the subtle signs of female interest that entices men to pursue a woman and also how to become more approachable to high-quality guys.

101 Reasons Why He Won't Commit To You: The Secret Fears, Doubts, And Insecurities That Prevent Most Men From Getting Married

In 101 Reasons Why He Won't Commit To You, you'll learn about the most common fears, doubts, and insecurities that paralyze men and prevent them from making the leap from boyfriend to husband.

More Great Books by Bruce Bryans:

If you have a special guy in your life that could use a bit more wisdom when it comes to dating and relating with women, you should sweetly suggest that he check out some of my books. Actually, even if YOU want to learn about what guys are learning about when it comes to understanding women, peruse through my other books listed below.

Attract The Right Girl: How To Find Your Perfect Girl And Make Her Chase You For A Relationship

In <u>Attract The Right Girl</u>, you'll discover how to find and choose an amazing girlfriend (who's perfect for you) and how to spark the kind of attraction that'll lead to a long-term relationship with her.

Find Your Path: A Short Guide To Living With Purpose And Being Your Own Man...No Matter What People Think

In <u>Find Your Path</u>, you'll discover how to find your mission in life and how to become a much more self-assured man of purpose and inner conviction.

How To Be A Better Boyfriend: The Relationship Manual For Becoming Mr. Right And Making A Woman Happy

In <u>How To Be A Better Boyfriend</u>, you'll discover how to cultivate a rock-solid, mind-blowing, romantic relationship with your dream girl, and what to do to avoid all the drama, bad girlfriend (or wife) behavior, and game playing that many "nice guys" often fall prey to in relationships.

How To Get Your Wife In The Mood: Quick And Easy Tips For Seducing Your Wife And Making Her BEG You For Sex

In How To Get Your Wife In The Mood, you'll discover the relationship secrets used by some of the most blissful couples in the world as well as romantic hacks that'll help you to get all the sex you want from your wife and make it seem like it was all HER idea.

Meet Her To Keep Her: The 10 Biggest Mistakes That Prevent Most Guys From Attracting And Keeping An Amazing Girlfriend

In Meet Her To Keep Her, you'll learn the ten dating mistakes that stop most guys from attracting and keeping a 'Total 10 girlfriend' and how to overcome them.

What Women Want In A Man: How To Become The Confident Man That Women Respect, Desire Sexually, And Want To Obey…In Every Way

In What Women Want In A Man, you'll learn how to become a high-quality, self-confident man that can naturally attract a good woman, maintain her sexual attraction to you, and keep her happy (and respectful) in a relationship.

Thank You

Before you go, I'd like to say "thank you" for purchasing my book.

I know you could have picked from dozens of books on understanding women, but you took a chance on my guide and for that I'm extremely grateful. So thanks again for purchasing this book and reading all the way to the end.

Now, IF you liked this book I'm going to need your help!

Please take a moment to leave a review for this book on Amazon. Your feedback will help me to continue to write the kind of Kindle books that helps you get results. And if you so happen to love this book, then please let me know!

20768126R00056

Printed in Poland
by Amazon Fulfillment
Poland Sp. z o.o., Wrocław